Leonardo Da Vinci

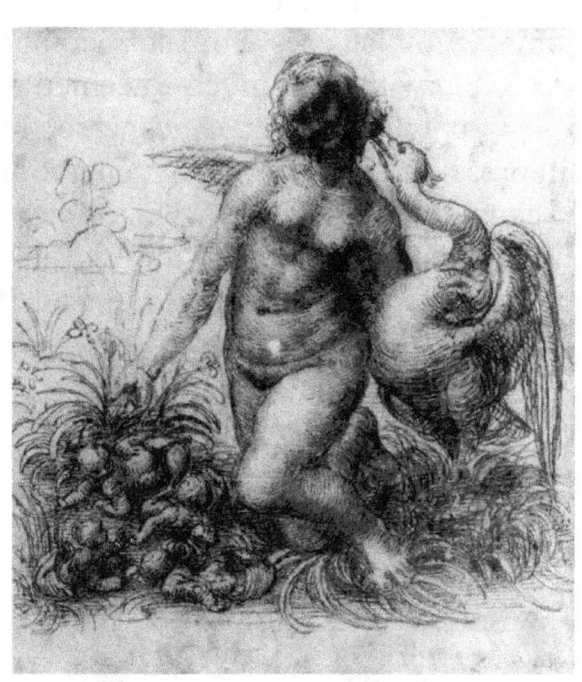

By Maurice W. Brockwell & Lacey Belinda Smith

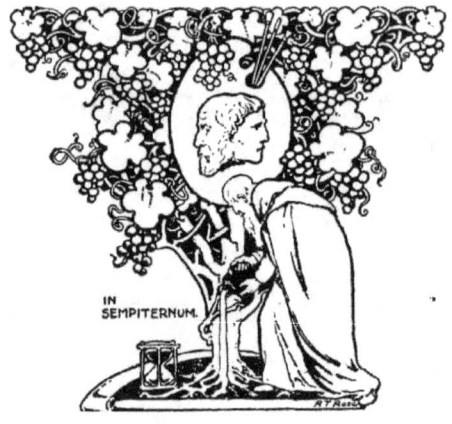

"Leonardo," wrote an English critic as far back as 1721, "was a Man so happy in his genius, so consummate in his Profession, so accomplished in the Arts, so knowing in the Sciences, and withal, so much esteemed by the Age wherein he lived, his Works so highly applauded by the Ages which have succeeded, and his Name and Memory still preserved with so much Veneration by the present Age— that, if anything could equal the Merit of the Man, it must be the Success he met with. Moreover, 'tis not in Painting alone, but in Philosophy, too, that Leonardo surpassed all his Brethren of the 'Pencil.'"

This admirable summary of the great Florentine painter's life's work still holds good to-day.

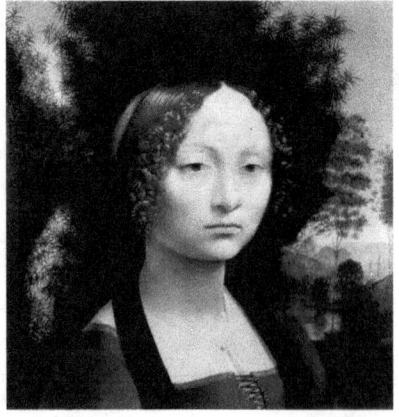

Portrait Of Ginevra Benci--1474

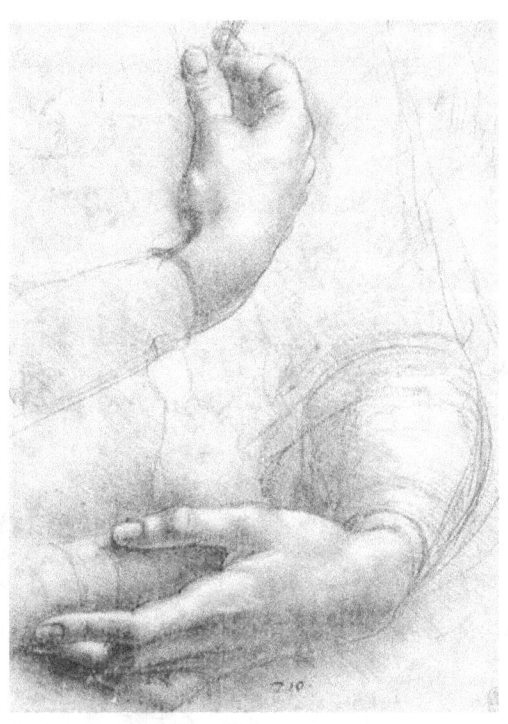

Study Of Hands--1474

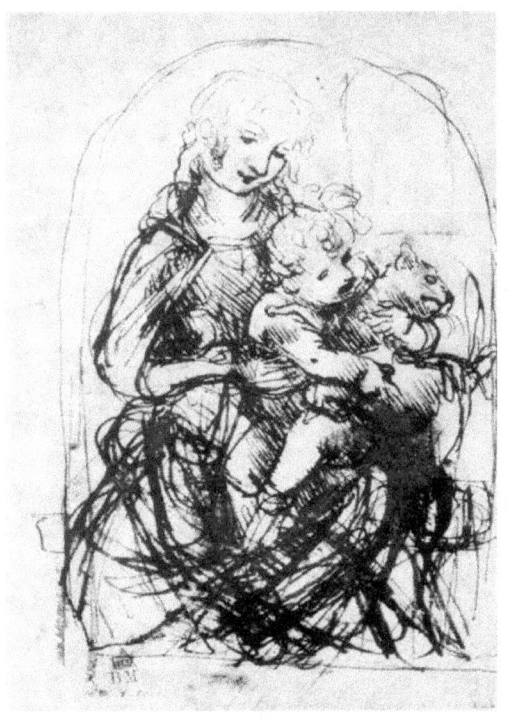

Study Of The Madonna And Child With A Cat-- 1478

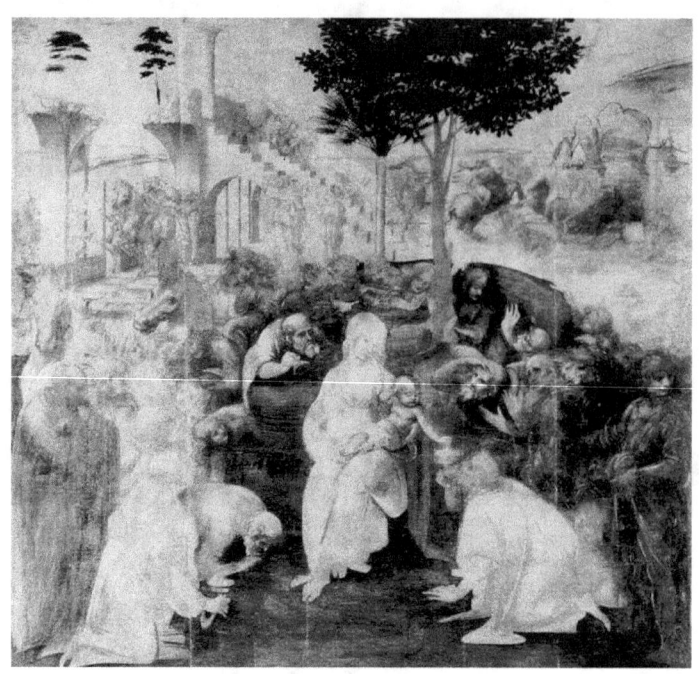

The Adoration Of The Magi-- 1480

Study For The Adoration Of The Magi--1480

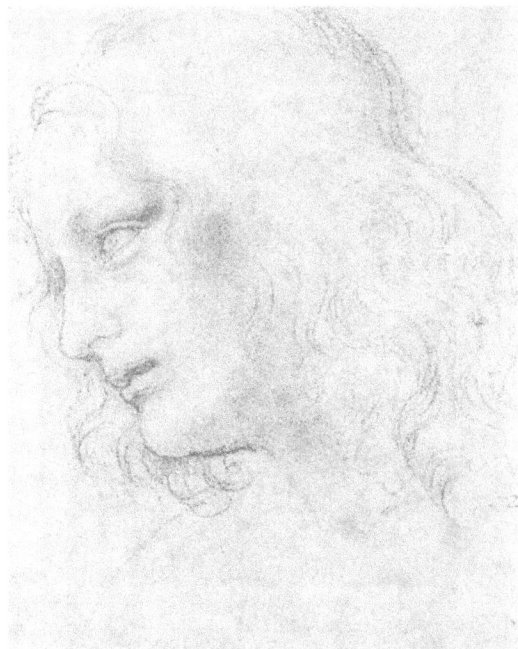

Study For The Last Supper: James--1495

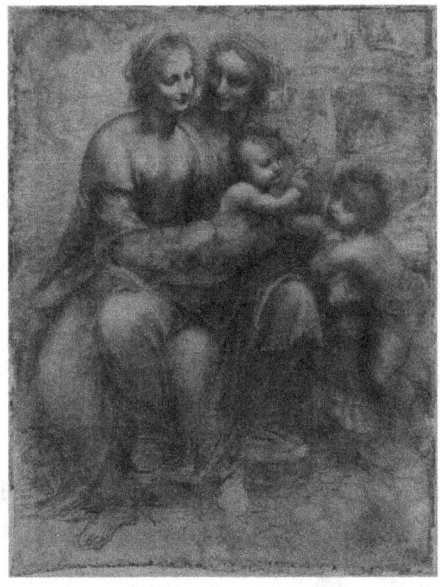

The Virgin And Child With Saint Anne And Saint John The Baptist--1499

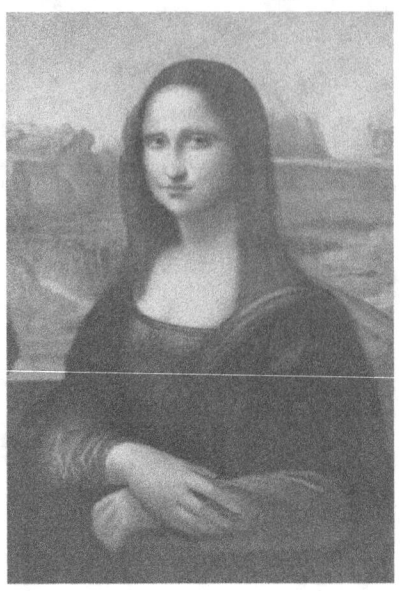

[I—MONA LISA. In the Louvre.]

Lisa del (1479 –1542),or Lisa Gherardini, or Lisa di Antonio Maria. The name of Mona Lisa was given to her portrait commissioned by her husband Leonardo da Vinci.

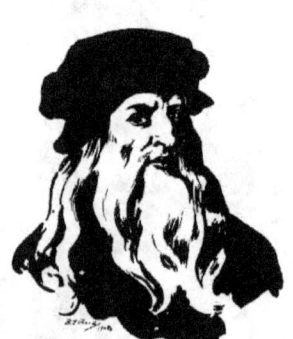

Leonardo da Vinci (1452–1519) was a great figure of the Italian Renaissance. He was an artist, sculptor, engineer, scientist and inventor.

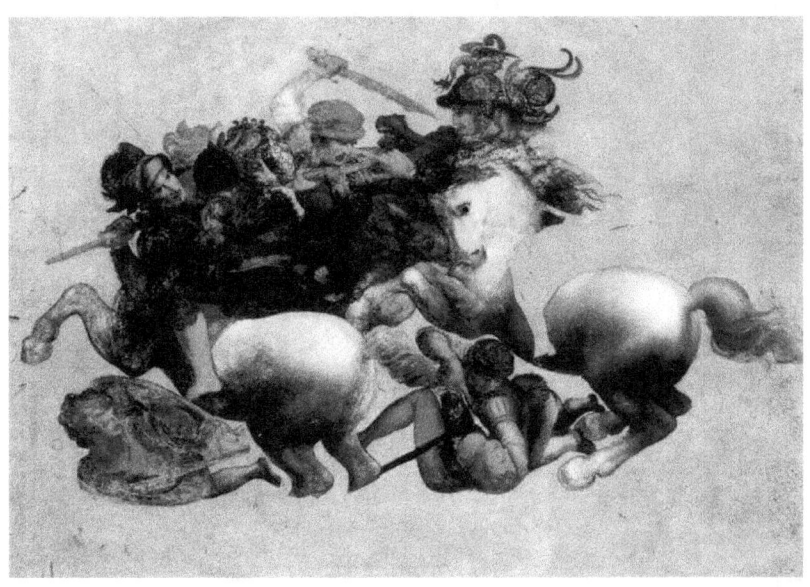

Battle Of Anghiari--1504

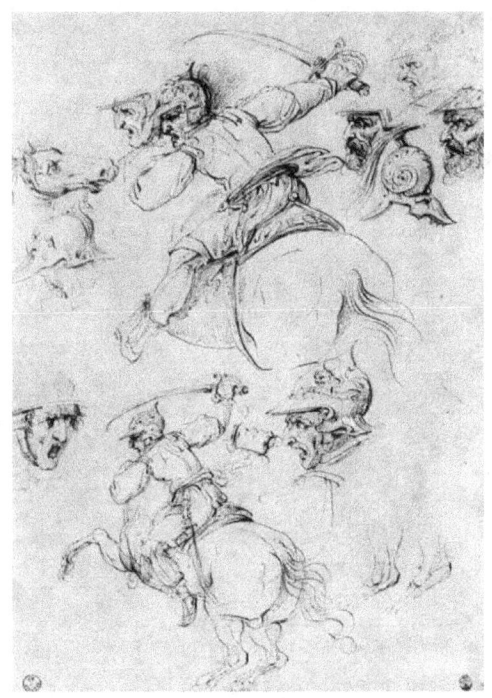

Study Of Battles On Horseback--1504

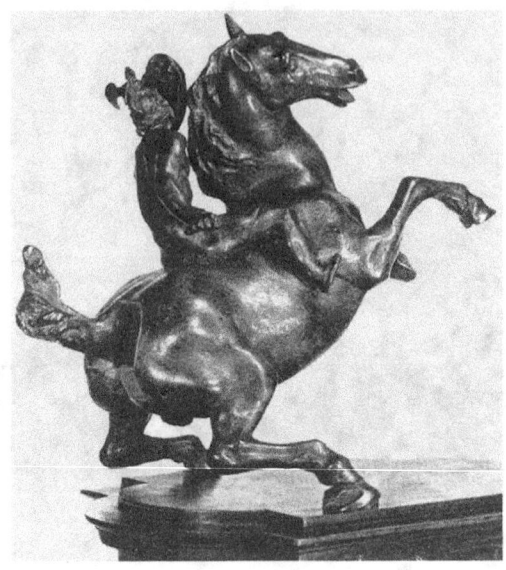

Equestrian Statue-- 1519

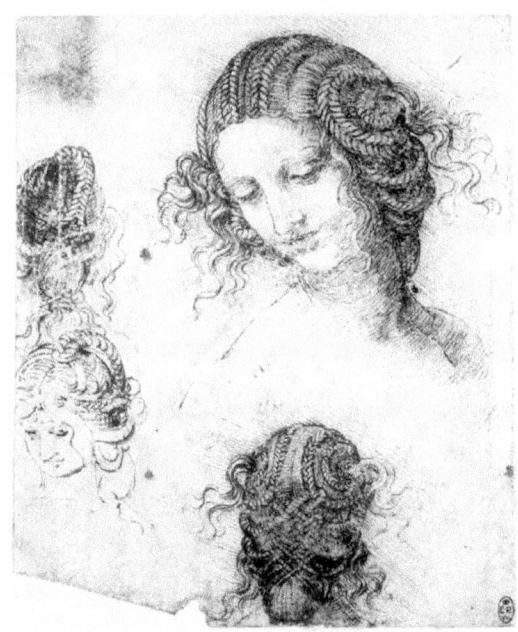

Head Of Leda--1505

In Greek mythology, Leda was the wife of king Tyndareus of Sparta. Her saga gave rise to the popular motif in Renaissance and later art of Leda and the Swan for she was admired by Zeus, who seduced her in the simulacrum of a swan.

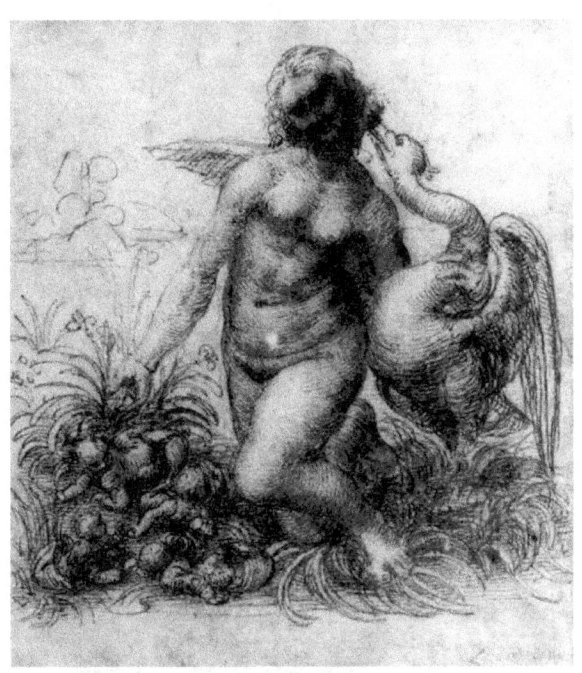

Leda And The Swan--1506

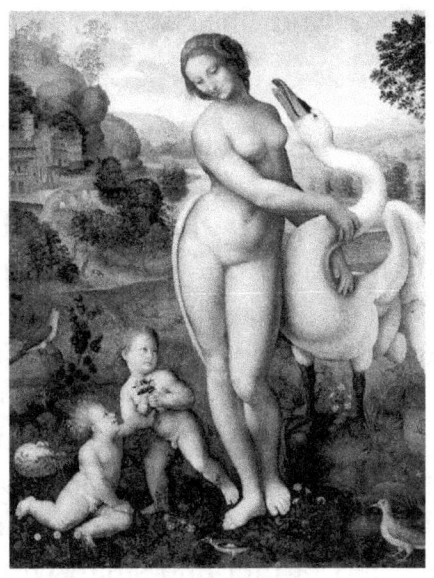

Leda--1510

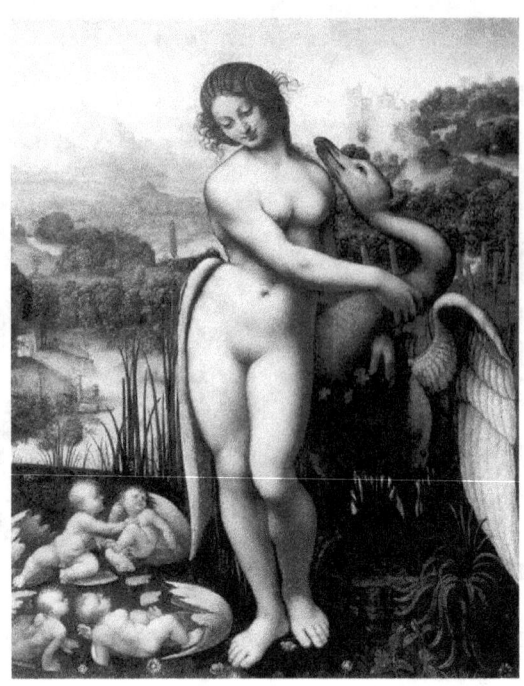

Leda And The Swan--1510

HIS BIRTH

Leonardo Da Vinci, the many-sided genius of the Italian Renaissance, was born, as his name implies, at the little town of Vinci, which is about six miles from Empoli and twenty miles west of Florence. Vinci is still very inaccessible, and the only means of conveyance is the cart of a general carrier and postman, who sets out on his journey from Empoli at sunrise and sunset. Outside a house in the middle of the main street of Vinci to-day a modern and white-washed bust of the great artist is pointed to with much pride by the inhabitants. Leonardo's traditional birthplace on the outskirts of the town still exists, and serves now as the headquarters of a farmer and small wine exporter.

Leonardo di Ser Piero d'Antonio di Ser Piero di Ser Guido da Vinci—for that was his full legal name—was the illegitimate son of a local lawyer Ser Piero, who, like his father, grandfather, and great-grandfather, followed that honourable vocation with distinction and success, and who subsequently—when Leonardo was a youth—was appointed notary to the Signoria of Florence. Leonardo's mother was one Caterina, who afterwards married Accabriga di Piero del Vaccha of Vinci.

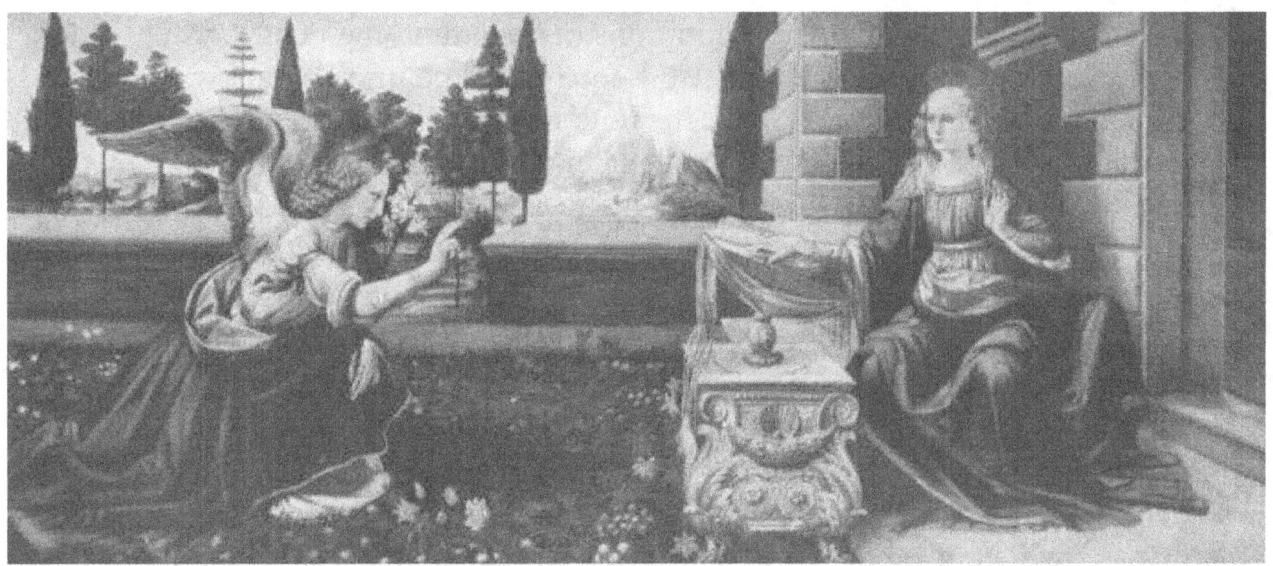

II.—Annunciation In the Uffizi Gallery, Florence. No. 1288. 3 ft 3 ins. By 6 ft 11 ins. (0.99 x 2.18)] Although this panel is included in the Uffizi Catalogue as being by Leonardo, it is in all probability by his master, Verrocchio.]

The date of Leonardo's birth is not known with any certainty. His age is given as five in a taxation return made in 1457 by his grandfather Antonio, in whose house he was educated; it is therefore concluded that he was born in 1452. Leonardo's father Ser Piero, who afterwards married four times, had eleven children by his third and fourth wives. Is it unreasonable to suggest that Leonardo may have had these numbers in mind in 1496-1498 when he was painting in his famous "Last Supper" the figures of eleven Apostles and one outcast?

However, Ser Piero seems to have legitimised his "love child" who very early showed promise of extraordinary talent and untiring energy.

HIS EARLY
TRAINING

Practically nothing is known about Leonardo's boyhood, but Vasari informs us that Ser Piero, impressed with the remarkable character of his son's genius, took some of his drawings to Andrea del Verrocchio, an intimate friend, and begged him earnestly to express an opinion on them. Verrocchio was so astonished at the power they revealed that he advised Ser Piero to send Leonardo to study under him. Leonardo thus entered the studio of Andrea del Verrocchio about 1469-1470. In the workshop of that great Florentine sculptor, goldsmith, and artist he met other craftsmen, metal workers, and youthful painters, among whom was Botticelli, at that moment of his development a jovial _habitué_ of the Poetical Supper Club, who had not yet given any premonitions of becoming the poet, mystic, and visionary of later times. There also Leonardo came into contact with that unoriginal painter Lorenzo di Credi, his junior by seven years. He also, no doubt, met Perugino, whom Michelangelo called "that blockhead in art." The genius and versatility of the Vincian painter was, however, in no way dulled by intercourse with lesser artists than himself; on the contrary he vied with each in turn, and readily outstripped his fellow pupils. In 1472, at the age of twenty, he was admitted into the Guild of Florentine Painters.

Unfortunately very few of Leonardo's paintings have come down to us. Indeed there do not exist a sufficient number of finished and absolutely authentic oil pictures from his own hand to afford illustrations for this short chronological sketch of his life's work. The few that do remain, however, are of so exquisite a quality—or were until they were "comforted" by the uninspired restorer—that we can unreservedly accept the enthusiastic records of tradition in respect of all his works. To rightly understand the essential characteristics of Leonardo's achievements it is necessary to regard him as a scientist quite as much as an artist, as a philosopher no less than a painter, and as a draughtsman rather than a colourist. There is hardly a branch of human learning to which he did not at one time or another give his eager attention, and he was engrossed in turn by the study of architecture—the foundation-stone of all true art—sculpture, mathematics, engineering and music. His versatility was unbounded, and we are apt to regret that this many-sided genius did not realise that it is by developing his power within certain limits that the great master is revealed. Leonardo may be described as the most Universal Genius of Christian times-perhaps of all time.

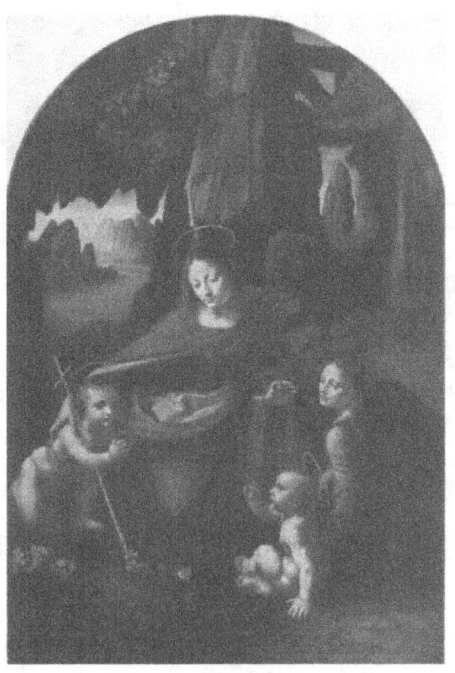

[III. THE VIRGIN OF THE ROCKS In the National Gallery. No. 1093. 6 ft. ½ in. h. by 3 ft 9 ½ in. w. (1.83 x 1.15)] This picture was painted in Milan about 1495 by Ambrogio da Predis under the supervision and guidance of Leonardo da Vinci, the essential features of the composition being borrowed from the earlier "Vierge aux Rochers," now in the Louvre.]

HIS EARLY WORKS

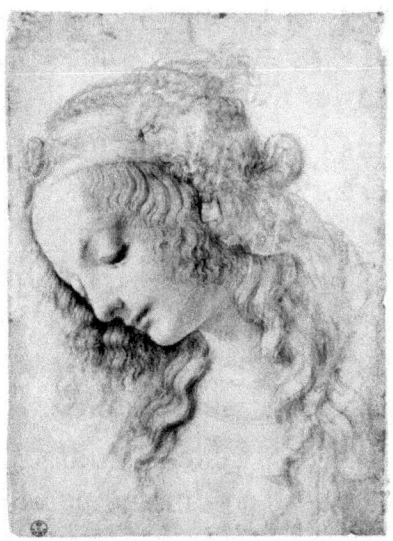

Woman's Head--1473

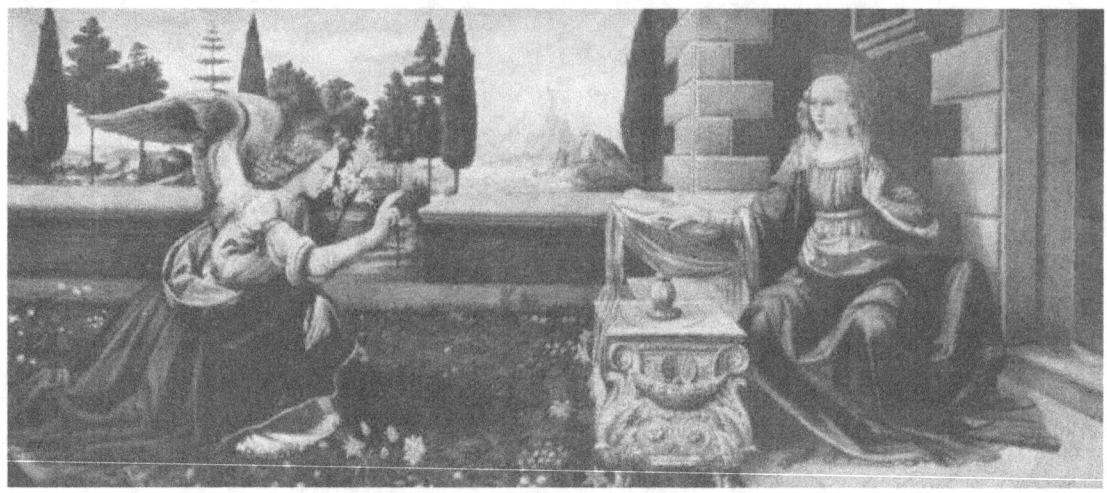

[II.—Annunciation In the Uffizi Gallery, Florence. No. 1288. 3 ft 3 ins. By 6 ft 11 ins. (0.99 x 2.18)]

To about the year 1472 belongs the small picture of the "Annunciation," now in the Louvre, which after being the subject of much contention among European critics has gradually won its way to general recognition as an early work by Leonardo himself. That it was painted in the studio of Verrocchio was always admitted, but it was long catalogued by the Louvre authorities under the name of Lorenzo di Credi. It is now, however, attributed to Leonardo (No. 1602 A). Such uncertainties as to attribution were common half a century ago when scientific art criticism was in its infancy.

Another painting of the "Annunciation," which is now in the Uffizi Gallery (No. 1288) is still officially attributed to Leonardo. This small picture, which has been considerably repainted, and is perhaps by Andrea del Verrocchio, Leonardo's master, is the subject of II.

To January 1473 belongs Leonardo's earliest dated work, a pen-and-ink drawing—"A Wide View over a Plain," now in the Uffizi. The inscription together with the date in the top left-hand corner is reversed, and proves a remarkable characteristic of Leonardo's handwriting—viz., that he wrote from right to left; indeed, it has been suggested that he did this in order to make it difficult for any one else to read the words, which were frequently committed to paper by the aid of peculiar abbreviations.

Leonardo continued to work in his master's studio till about 1477. On January 1st of the following year, 1478, he was commissioned to paint an altar-piece for the Chapel of St. Bernardo in the Palazzo Vecchio, and he was paid twenty-five florins on account. He, however, never carried out the work, and after waiting five years the Signoria transferred the commission to Domenico Ghirlandajo, who also failed to accomplish the task, which was ultimately, some seven years later, completed by

Filippino Lippi. This panel of the "Madonna Enthroned, St. Victor, St. John Baptist, St. Bernard, and St. Zenobius," which is dated February 20, 1485, is now in the Uffizi.

That Leonardo was by this time a facile draughtsman is evidenced by his vigorous pen-and-ink sketch—now in a private collection in Paris—of Bernardo Bandini, who in the Pazzi Conspiracy of April 1478 stabbed Giuliano de' Medici to death in the Cathedral at Florence during High Mass. The drawing is dated December 29, 1479, the date of Bandini's public execution in Florence.

In that year also, no doubt, was painted the early and, as might be expected, unfinished "St. Jerome in the Desert," now in the Vatican, the under-painting being in umber and _terraverte_. Its authenticity is vouched for not only by the internal evidence of the picture itself, but also by the similarity of treatment seen in a drawing in the Royal Library at Windsor. Cardinal Fesch, a princely collector in Rome in the early part of the nineteenth century, found part of the picture—the torso—being used as a box-cover in a shop in Rome. He long afterwards discovered in a shoemaker's shop a panel of the head which belonged to the torso. The jointed panel was eventually purchased by Pope Pius IX., and added to the Vatican Collection.

In March 1480 Leonardo was commissioned to paint an altar-piece for the monks of St. Donato at Scopeto, for which payment in advance was made to him. That he intended to carry out this contract seems most probable. He, however, never completed the picture, although it gave rise to the supremely beautiful cartoon of the "Adoration of the Magi," now in the Uffizi (No. 1252). As a matter of course it is unfinished, only the under-painting and the colouring of the figures in green on a brown ground having been executed. The rhythm of line, the variety of attitude, the profound feeling for landscape and an early application of chiaroscuro effect combine to render this one of his most characteristic productions.

Vasari tells us that while Verrocchio was painting the "Baptism of Christ" he allowed Leonardo to paint in one of the attendant angels holding some vestments. This the pupil did so admirably that his remarkable genius clearly revealed itself, the angel which Leonardo painted being much better than the portion executed by his master. This "Baptism of Christ," which is now in the Accademia in Florence and is in a bad state of preservation, appears to have been a comparatively early work by Verrocchio, and to have been painted in 1480-1482, when Leonardo would be about thirty years of age.

To about this period belongs the superb drawing of the "Warrior," now in the Malcolm Collection in the British Museum. This drawing may have been made while Leonardo still frequented the studio of Andrea del Verrocchio, who in 1479 was commissioned to execute the equestrian statue of Bartolommeo Colleoni, which was completed twenty years later and still adorns the Campo di San Giovanni e Paolo in Venice.

FIRST VISIT TO
MILAN

About 1482 Leonardo entered the service of Ludovico Sforza, having first written to his future patron a full statement of his various abilities in the following terms:—

"Having, most illustrious lord, seen and pondered over the experiments made by those who pass as masters in the art of inventing instruments of war, and having satisfied myself that they in no way differ from those in general use, I make so bold as to solicit, without prejudice to any one, an opportunity of informing your excellency of some of my own secrets."

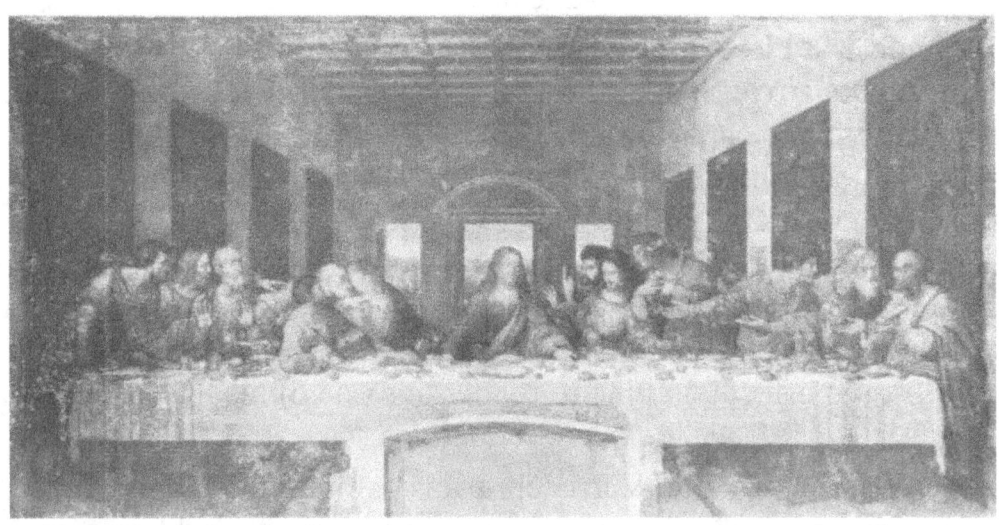

[IV.-THE LAST SUPPER Refectory of St. Maria delle Grazie, Milan. About 13 feet 8 ins. h. by 26 ft. 7 ins. w. (4.16 x 8.09)]

He goes on to say that he can construct light bridges which can be transported, that he can make pontoons and scaling ladders, that he can construct cannon and mortars unlike those commonly used, as well as catapults and other engines of war; or if the fight should take place at sea that he can build engines which shall be suitable alike for defence as for attack, while in time of peace he can erect public and private buildings. Moreover, he urges that he can also execute sculpture in marble, bronze, or clay, and, with regard to painting, "can do as well as any one else, no matter who he may be." In conclusion, he offers to execute the proposed bronze equestrian statue of Francesco Sforza "which shall bring glory and never-ending honour to that illustrious house."

It was about 1482, the probable date of Leonardo's migration from Florence to Milan, that he painted the "Vierge aux Rochers," now in the Louvre (No. 1599). It is an essentially Florentine picture, and although it has no pedigree earlier than 1625, when it was in the Royal Collection at Fontainebleau, it is undoubtedly much earlier and considerably more authentic than the "Virgin of the Rocks," now in the National Gallery (III.).

He certainly set to work about this time on the projected statue of Francesco Sforza, but probably then made very little progress with it. He may also in that year or the next have painted the lost portrait of Cecilia Gallerani, one of the mistresses of Ludovico Sforza. It has, however, been surmised that that lady's features are preserved to us in the "Lady with a Weasel," by Leonardo's pupil Boltraffio, which is now in the Czartoryski Collection at Cracow.

IN THE EAST

The absence of any record of Leonardo in Milan, or elsewhere in Italy, between 1483 and 1487 has led critics to the conclusion, based on documentary evidence of a somewhat complicated nature, that he spent those years in the service of the Sultan of Egypt, travelling in Armenia and the East as his engineer.

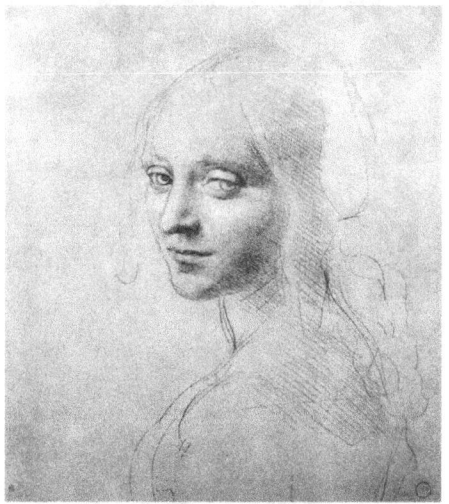

Head Of A Girl--1483

BACK IN MILAN

In 1487 he was again resident in Milan as general artificer—using that term in its widest sense—to Ludovico. Among his various activities at this period must be mentioned the designs he made for the cupola of the cathedral at Milan, and the scenery he constructed for "Il Paradiso," which was written by Bernardo Bellincioni on the occasion of the marriage of Gian Galeazzo with Isabella of Aragon. About 1489-1490 he began his celebrated "Treatise on Painting" and recommenced work on the colossal equestrian statue of Francesco Sforza, which was doubtless the greatest of all his achievements as a sculptor. It was, however, never cast in bronze, and was ruthlessly destroyed by the French bowmen in April 1500, on their occupation of Milan after the defeat of Ludovico at the battle of Novara. This is all the more regrettable as no single authentic piece of sculpture has come down to us from Leonardo's hand, and we can only judge of his power in this direction from his drawings, and the enthusiastic praise of his contemporaries.

This copy is usually ascribed to Marco d'Oggiono, but some critics claim that it is by Gianpetrino. It is the same size as the original.]

THE VIRGIN OF
THE ROCKS

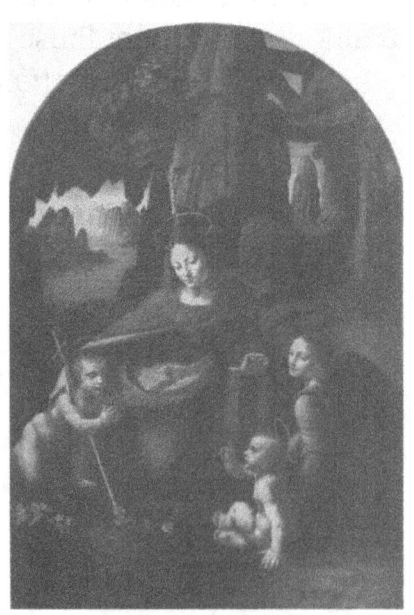

The "Virgin of the Rocks" (III.), now in the National Gallery, corresponds exactly with a painting by Leonardo which was described by Lomazzo about 1584 as being in the Chapel of the Conception in the Church of St. Francesco at Milan. This picture, the only _oeuvre_ in this gallery with which Leonardo's name can be connected, was brought to England in 1777 by Gavin Hamilton, and sold by him to the Marquess of Lansdowne, who subsequently exchanged it for another picture in the Collection of the Earl of Suffolk at Charlton Park, Wiltshire, from whom it was eventually purchased by the National Gallery for £9000. Signor Emilio Motta, some fifteen years ago, unearthed in the State Archives of Milan a letter or memorial from Giovanni Ambrogio da Predis and Leonardo da Vinci to the Duke of Milan, praying him to intervene in a dispute, which had arisen between the petitioners and the Brotherhood of the Conception, with regard to the valuation of certain works of art furnished for the chapel of the Brotherhood in the church of St. Francesco. The only logical deduction which can be drawn from documentary evidence is that the "Vierge aux Rochers" in the Louvre is the picture, painted about 1482, which between 1491 and 1494 gave rise to the dispute, and that, when it was ultimately sold by the artists for the full price asked to some unknown buyer, the National Gallery version was executed for a smaller price mainly by Ambrogio da Predisunder the supervision, and with the help, of Leonardo to be placed in the Chapel of the Conception.

The differences between the earlier, the more authentic, and the more characteristically Florentine "Vierge aux Rochers," in the Louvre, and the "Virgin of the Rocks," in the National Gallery, are that in the latter picture the hand of the angel, seated by the side of the Infant Christ, is raised and pointed in the direction of the little St. John the Baptist; that the St John has a reed cross and the three principal figures have gilt nimbi, which were, however, evidently added much later. In the National Gallery version the left hand of the Madonna, the Christ's right hand and arm, and the forehead of St. John the Baptist are freely restored, while a strip of the foreground right across the whole picture is ill painted and lacks accent. The head of the angel is, however, magnificently painted, and by Leonardo; the panel, taken as a whole, is exceedingly beautiful and full of charm and tenderness.

THE LAST
SUPPER

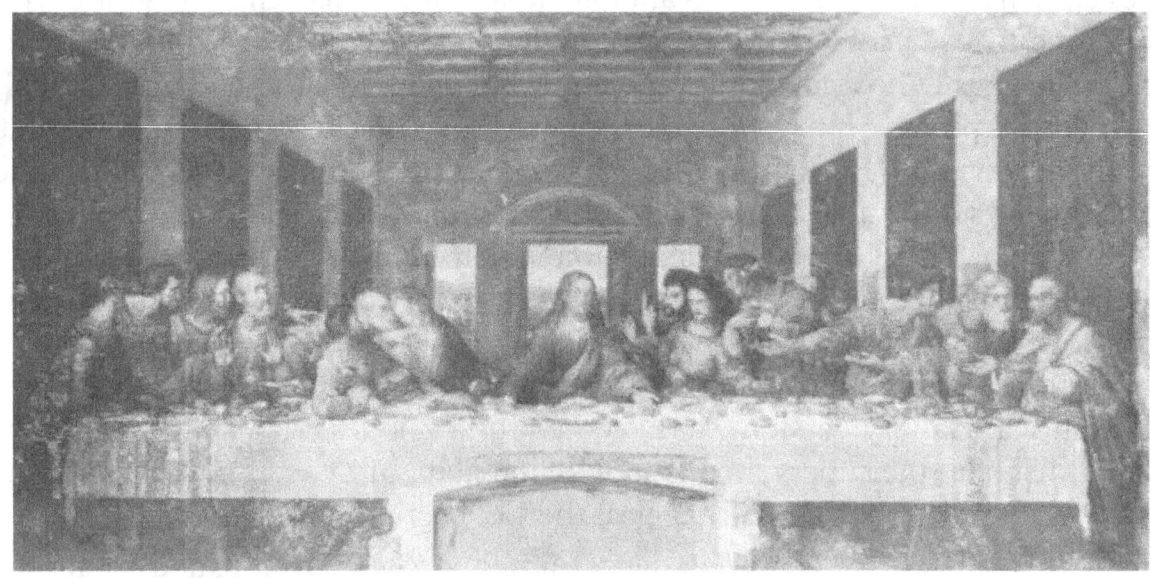

Between 1496 and 1498 Leonardo painted his _chef d'oeuvre_, the "Last Supper," (IV.) for the end wall of the Refectory of the Dominican Convent of S. Maria delle Grazie at Milan. It was originally executed in tempera on a badly prepared stucco ground and began to deteriorate a very few years after its completion. As early as 1556 it was half ruined. In 1652 the monks cut away a part of the fresco including the feet of the Christ to make a doorway. In 1726 one Michelangelo Belotti, an obscure Milanese painter, received £300 for the worthless labour he bestowed on restoring it. He seems to have employed some astringent restorative which revived the colours temporarily, and then left them in deeper eclipse than before. In 1770 the fresco was again restored by Mazza. In 1796 Napoleon's cavalry, contrary to his express orders, turned the refectory into a stable, and pelted the heads of the figures with dirt. Subsequently the refectory was used to store hay, and at one time or another it has been flooded. In 1820 the fresco was again restored, and in 1854 this restoration was effaced. In October 1908

Professor Cavenaghi completed the delicate task of again restoring it, and has, in the opinion of experts, now preserved it from further injury. In addition, the devices of Ludovico and his Duchess and a considerable amount of floral decoration by Leonardo himself have been brought to light.

Leonardo has succeeded in producing the effect of the _coup de théâtre_ at the moment when Jesus said "One of you shall betray me." Instantly the various apostles realise that there is a traitor among their number, and show by their different gestures their different passions, and reveal their different temperaments. On the left of Christ is St. John who is overcome with grief and is interrogated by the impetuous Peter, near whom is seated Judas Iscariot who, while affecting the calm of innocence, is quite unable to conceal his inner feelings; he instinctively clasps the money-bag and in so doing upsets the salt-cellar.

It will be remembered that the Prior of the Convent complained to Ludovico Sforza, Duke of Milan, that Leonardo was taking too long to paint the fresco and was causing the Convent considerable inconvenience. Leonardo had his revenge by threatening to paint the features of the impatient Prior into the face of Judas Iscariot. The incident has been quaintly told in the following lines:—

"Padre Bandelli, then, complains of me   Because, forsooth, I have not drawn a line   Upon the Saviour's head; perhaps, then, he   Could without trouble paint that head divine.   But think, oh Signor Duca, what should be   The pure perfection of Our Saviour's face—   What sorrowing majesty, what noble grace,   At that dread moment when He brake the bread,   And those submissive words of pathos said:

"'By one among you I shall be betrayed,'—   And say if 'tis an easy task to find Even among the best that walk this Earth,   The fitting type of that divinest worth, That has its image solely in the mind.   Vainly my pencil struggles to express The sorrowing grandeur of such holiness.   In patient thought, in ever-seeking prayer,   I strive to shape that glorious face within,   But the soul's mirror, dulled and dimmed by sin,   Reflects not yet the perfect image there.   Can the hand do before the soul has wrought;   Is not our art the servant of our thought?

"And Judas too, the basest face I see,   Will not contain his utter infamy; Among the dregs and offal of mankind   Vainly I seek an utter wretch to find. He who for thirty silver coins could sell   His Lord, must be the Devil's miracle. Padre Bandelli thinks it easy is   To find the type of him who with a kiss Betrayed his Lord. Well, what I can I'll do;   And if it please his reverence and you,   For Judas' face I'm willing to paint his."

"... I dare not paint   Till all is ordered and matured within,   Hand-work and head-work have an earthly taint,   But when the soul commands I shall begin;   On themes like these I should not dare to dwell   With our good Prior—they to him would be   Mere nonsense; he must touch and taste and see,   And facts, he says, are never mystical."

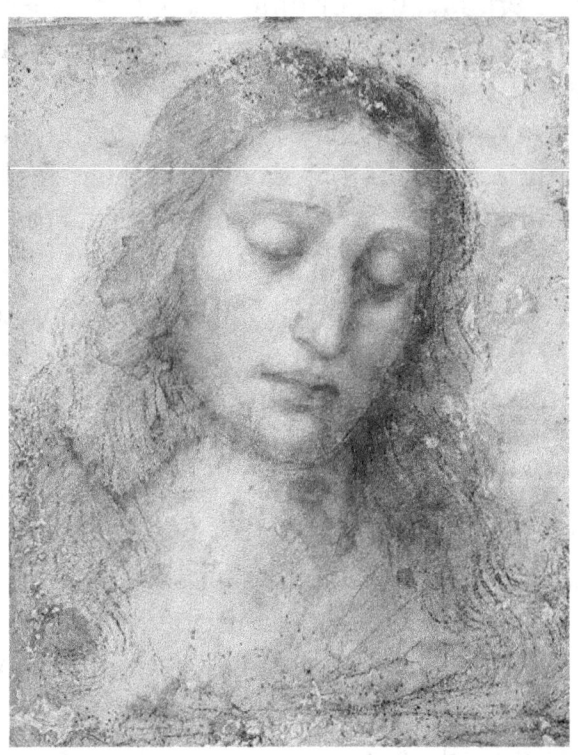

[VI.—THE HEAD OF CHRIST In the Brera Gallery, Milan. No. 280. 1 ft. 0-1/2 ins. by 1 ft. 4 ins. (0.32 x 0.40)]

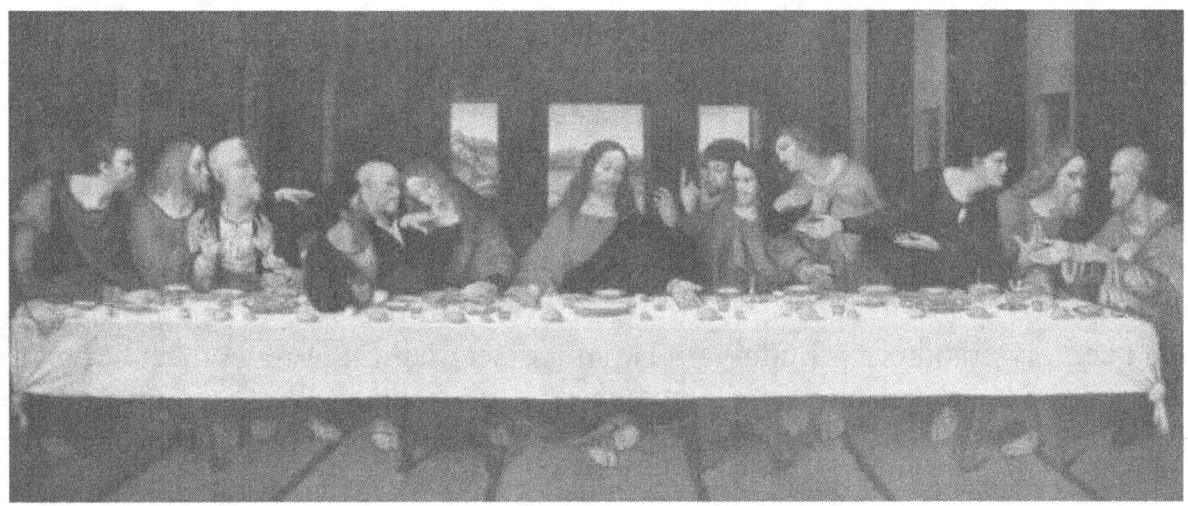

The copy of the "Last Supper" (V.) by Marco d'Oggiono, now in the Diploma Gallery at Burlington House, was made shortly after the original painting was completed. It gives but a faint echo of that sublime work "in which the ideal and the real were blended in perfect unity." This copy was long in the possession of the Carthusians in their Convent at Pavia, and, on the suppression of that Order and the sale of their effects in 1793, passed into the possession of a grocer at Milan. It was subsequently purchased for £600 by the Royal Academy on the advice of Sir Thomas Lawrence, who left no stone unturned to acquire also the original studies for the heads of the Apostles. Some of these in red and black chalk are now preserved in the Royal Library at Windsor, where there are in all 145 drawings by Leonardo.

Several other old copies of the fresco exist, notably the one in the Louvre. Francis I. wished to remove the whole wall of the Refectory to Paris, but he was persuaded that that would be impossible; the Constable de Montmorency then had a copy made for the Chapel of the Château d'Ecouen, whence it ultimately passed to the Louvre.

The singularly beautiful "Head of Christ" (VI.), now in the Brera Gallery at Milan, is the original study for the head of the principal figure in the fresco painting of the "Last Supper." In spite of decay and restoration it expresses "the most elevated seriousness together with Divine Gentleness, pain on account of the faithlessness of His disciples, a full presentiment of His own death, and resignation to the will of His Father."

THE COURT OF
MILAN

Ludovico, to whom Leonardo was now court-painter, had married Beatrice d'Este, in 1491, when she was only fifteen years of age. The young Duchess, who at one time owned as many as eighty-four splendid gowns, refused to wear a certain dress of woven gold, which her husband had given her, if Cecilia Gallerani, the Sappho of her day, continued to wear a very similar one, which presumably had been given to her by Ludovico. Having discarded Cecilia, who, as her tastes did not lie in the direction of the Convent, was married in 1491 to Count Ludovico Bergamini, the Duke in 1496 became enamoured of Lucrezia Crivelli, a lady-in-waiting to the Duchess Beatrice.

Leonardo, as court painter, perhaps painted a portrait, now lost, of Lucrezia, whose features are more likely to be preserved to us in the portrait by Ambrogio da Predis, now in the Collection of the Earl of Roden, than in the quite unauthenticated portrait (VII.), now in the Louvre (No. 1600).

On January 2, 1497, Beatrice spent three hours in prayer in the church of St. Maria delle Grazie, and the same night gave birth to a stillborn child. In a few hours she passed away, and from that moment Ludovico was a changed man. He went daily to see her tomb, and was quite overcome with grief.

In April 1498, Isabella d'Este, Beatrice's elder, more beautiful, and more graceful sister, "at the sound of whose name all the muses rise and do reverence" wrote to Cecilia Gallerani, or Bergamini, asking her to lend her the portrait which Leonardo had painted of her some fifteen years earlier, as she wished to compare it with a picture by Giovanni Bellini. Cecilia graciously lent the picture—now presumably lost—adding her regret that it no longer resembled her.

LEONARDO
LEAVES MILAN

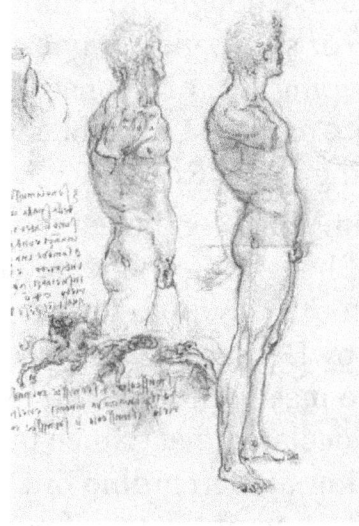

The Anatomy Of A Male Nude And A Battle Scene--1505

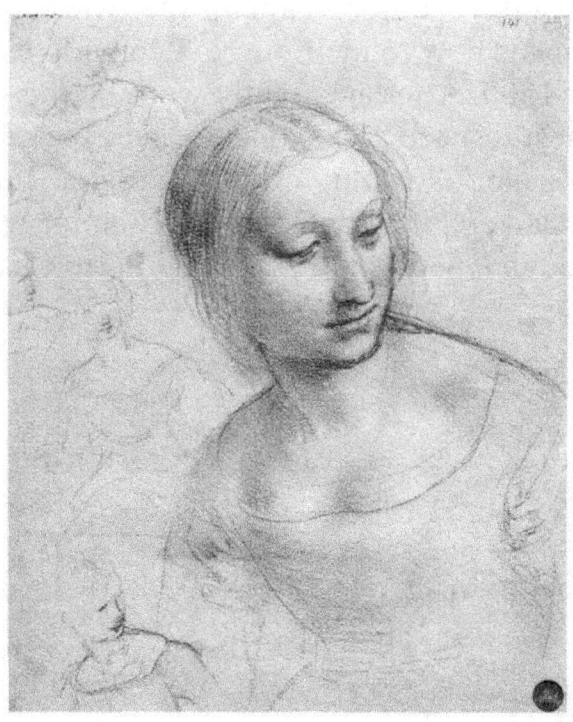

Study For Madonna With The Yarnwinder-- 1501

Among the last of Leonardo da Vinci's works in Milan towards the end of 1499 was, probably, the superb cartoon of "The Virgin and Child with St. Anne and St. John," now at Burlington House. Though little known to the general public, this large drawing on _carton_, or stiff paper, is one of the greatest of London's treasures, as it reveals the sweeping line of Leonardo's powerful draughtsmanship. It was in the Pompeo Leoni, Arconati, Casnedi, and Udney Collections before passing to the Royal Academy.

In 1499 the stormy times in Milan foreboded the end of Ludovico's reign. In April of that year we read of his giving a vineyard to Leonardo; in September Ludovico had to leave Milan for the Tyrol to raise an army, and on the 14th of the same month the city was sold by Bernardino di Corte to the French, who occupied it from 1500 to 1512. Ludovico may well have had in mind the figure of the traitor in the "Last Supper" when he declared that "Since the days of Judas Iscariot there has never been so black a traitor as Bernardino di Corte." On October 6th Louis XII. entered the city. Before the end of the year Leonardo, realising the necessity for his speedy departure, sent six hundred gold florins by letter of exchange to Florence to be placed to his credit with the hospital of S. Maria Nuova.

In the following year, Ludovico having been defeated at Novara, Leonardo was a homeless wanderer. He left Milan for Mantua, where he drew a portrait in chalk of Isabella d'Este, which is now in the Louvre. Leonardo eventually arrived in Florence about Easter 1500. After apparently working there in 1501 on a second Cartoon, similar in most respects to the one he had executed in Milan two years earlier, he travelled in Umbria, visiting Orvieto, Pesaro, Rimini, and other towns, acting as engineer and architect to Cesare Borgia, for whom he planned a navigable canal between Cesena and Porto Cese-natico.

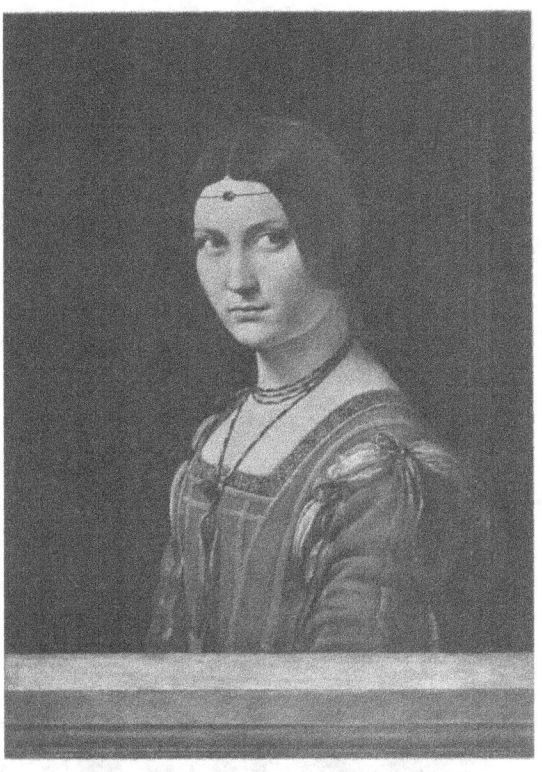

[VII.-PORTRAIT (PRESUMED) OF LUCREZIA CRIVELLI In the Louvre. No. 1600 [483]. 2 ft by I ft 5 ins. (0.62 x 0.44) This picture, although officially attributed to Leonardo, is probably not by him, and almost certainly does not represent Lucrezia Crivelli. It was once known as a "Portrait of a Lady" and is still occasionally miscalled "La Belle Féronnière."]

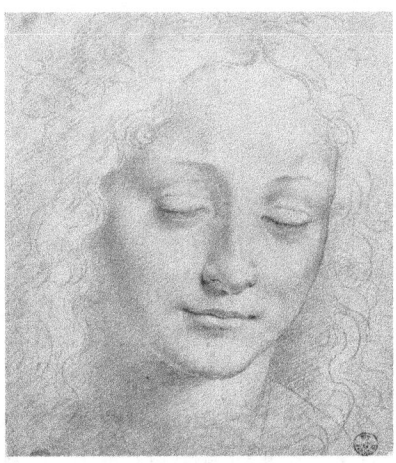

Female Head

MONA LISA

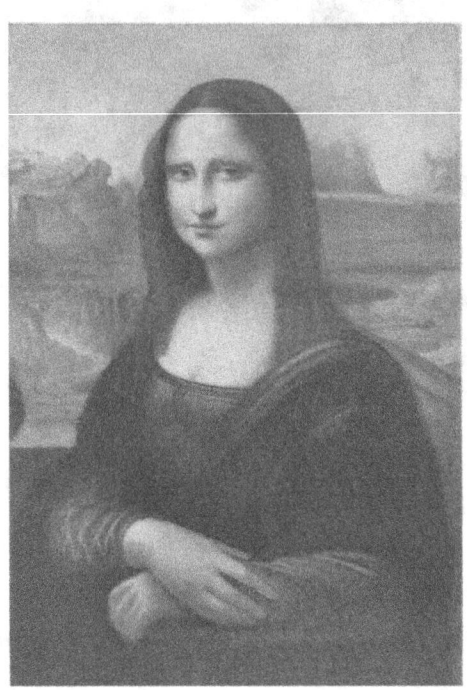

Early in 1503 he was back again in Florence, and set to work in earnest on the "Portrait of Mona Lisa" (I.), now in the Louvre (No. 1601). Lisa di Anton Maria di Noldo Gherardini was the daughter of Antonio Gherardini. In 1495 she married Francesco di Bartolommeo de Zenobi del Giocondo. It is from the surname of her husband that she derives the name of "La Joconde," by which her portrait is officially known in the Louvre. Vasari is probably inaccurate in saying that Leonardo "loitered over it for four years, and finally left it unfinished." He may have begun it in the spring of 1501 and, probably owing to having taken service under Cesare Borgia in the following year, put it on one side, ultimately completing it after working on the "Battle of Anghiari" in 1504. Vasari's eulogy of this portrait may with advantage be quoted: "Whoever shall desire to see how far art can imitate nature may do so to perfection in this head, wherein every peculiarity that could be depicted by the utmost subtlety of the pencil has been faithfully reproduced. The eyes have the lustrous brightness and moisture which is seen in life, and around them are those pale, red, and slightly livid circles, also proper to nature. The nose, with its beautiful and delicately roseate nostrils, might be easily believed to be alive; the mouth, admirable in its outline, has the lips uniting the rose-tints of their colour with those of the face, in the utmost perfection, and the carnation of the cheek does not appear to be painted, but truly flesh and blood. He who looks earnestly at the pit of the throat cannot but believe that he sees the beating of the pulses. Mona Lisa was exceedingly beautiful, and while Leonardo was painting her portrait, he took the precaution of keeping some one constantly near her to sing or play on instruments, or to jest and otherwise amuse her."

Leonardo painted this picture in the full maturity of his talent, and, although it is now little more than a monochrome owing to the free and merciless restoration to which it has been at times subjected, it must have created a wonderful impression on those who saw it in the early years of the sixteenth century. It is difficult for the unpractised eye to-day to form any idea of its original beauty. Leonardo has here painted this worldly-minded woman—her portrait is much more famous than she herself ever was—with a marvellous charm and suavity, a finesse of expression never reached before and hardly ever equalled since. Contrast the head of the Christ at Milan, Leonardo's conception of divinity expressed in perfect humanity, with the subtle and sphinx-like smile of this languorous creature.

The landscape background, against which Mona Lisa is posed, recalls the severe, rather than exuberant, landscape and the dim vistas of mountain ranges seen in the neighbourhood of his own birthplace. The portrait was bought during the reign of Francis I. for a sum which is to-day equal to about £1800. Leonardo, by the way, does not seem to have been really affected by any individual affection for any woman, and, like Michelangelo and Raphael, never married.

In January 4, 1504, Leonardo was one of the members of the Committee of Artists summoned to advise the Signoria as to the most suitable site for the erection of Michelangelo's statue of "David," which had recently been completed.

BATTLE OF
ANGHIARI

In the following May he was commissioned by the Signoria to decorate one of the walls of the Council Hall of the Palazzo Vecchio. The subject he selected was the "Battle of Anghiari." Although he completed the cartoon, the only part of the composition which he eventually executed in colour was an incident in the foreground which dealt with the "Battle of the Standard." One of the many supposed copies of a study of this mural painting now hangs on the south-east staircase in the Victoria and Albert Museum. It depicts the Florentines under Cardinal Ludovico Mezzarota Scarampo fighting against the Milanese under Niccolò Piccinino, the General of Filippo Maria Visconti, on June 29, 1440.

AGAIN IN MILAN

Leonardo was back in Milan in May 1506 in the service of the French King, for whom he executed, apparently with the help of assistants, "the Madonna, the Infant Christ, and Saint Anne" (VIII.). The composition of this oil-painting seems to have been built up on the second cartoon, which he had made some eight years earlier, and which was apparently taken to France in 1516 and ultimately lost.

IN ROME

From 1513-1515 he was in Rome, where Giovanni de' Medici had been elected Pope under the title of Leo X. He did not, however, work for the Pope, although he resided in the Vatican, his time being occupied in studying acoustics, anatomy, optics, geology, minerals, engineering, and geometry!

IN FRANCE

At last in 1516, three years before his death, Leonardo left his native land for France, where he received from Francis I. a princely income. His powers, however, had already begun to fail, and he produced very little in the country of his adoption. It is, nevertheless, only in the Louvre that his achievements as a painter can to-day be adequately studied.

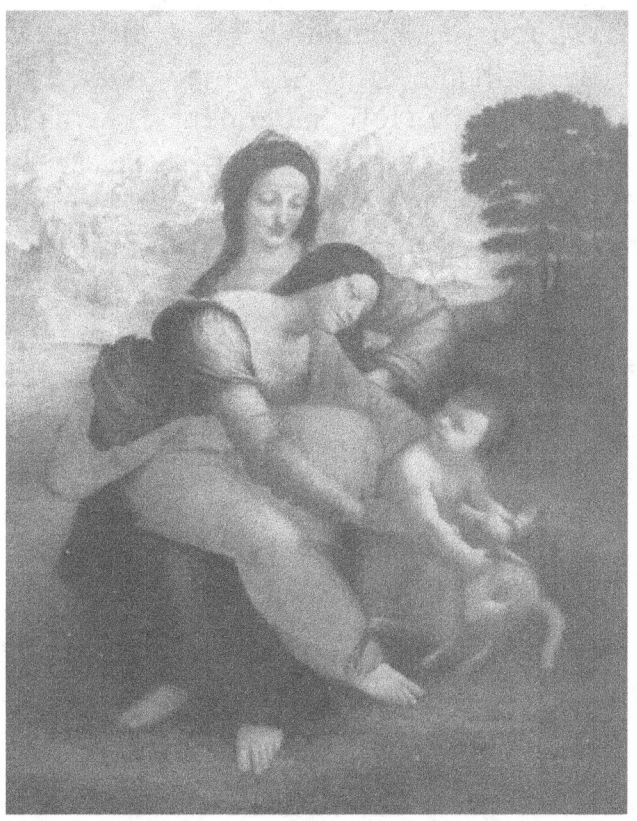

[VIII.-MADONNA, INFANT CHRIST, AND ST. ANNE In the Louvre. No. 1508. 5 ft. 7 in. h. by 4 ft. 3 in. w. (1.70 x 1.29) Painted between 1509 and 1516 with the help of assistants.]

On October 10, 1516, when he was resident at the Manor House of Cloux near Amboise in Touraine with Francesco Melzi, his friend and assistant, he showed three of his pictures to the Cardinal of Aragon, but his right hand was now paralysed, and he could "no longer colour with that sweetness with which he was wont, although still able to make drawings and to teach others."

It was no doubt in these closing years of his life that he drew the "Portrait of Himself" in red chalk, now at Turin, which is probably the only authentic portrait of him in existence.

HIS DEATH

On April 23, 1519—Easter Eve—exactly forty-five years before the birth of Shakespeare, Leonardo da Vinci made his will, and on May 2 of the same year he passed away.

Vasari informs us that Leonardo, "having become old, lay sick for many months, and finding himself near death and being sustained in the arms of his servants and friends, devoutly received the Holy Sacrament. He was then seized with a paroxysm, the forerunner of death, when King Francis I., who was accustomed frequently and affectionately to visit him, rose and supported his head to give him such assistance and to do him such favour as he could in the hope of alleviating his sufferings. The spirit of Leonardo, which was most divine, conscious that he could attain to no greater honour, departed in the arms of the monarch, being at that time in the seventy-fifth year of his age." The not over-veracious chronicler, however, is here drawing largely upon his imagination. Leonardo was only sixty-seven years of age, and the King was in all probability on that date at St. Germain-en Laye!

Thus died "Mr. Lionard de Vincy, the noble Milanese, painter, engineer, and architect to the King, State Mechanician" and "former Professor of Painting to the Duke of Milan."

"May God Almighty grant him His eternal peace," wrote his friend and assistant Francesco Melzi. "Every one laments the loss of a man whose like Nature cannot produce a second time."

HIS ART

Leonardo, whose birth antedates that of Michelangelo and Raphael by twenty three and thirty-one years respectively, was thus in the forefront of the Florentine Renaissance, his life coinciding almost exactly with the best period of Tuscan painting.

Leonardo was the first to investigate scientifically and to apply to art the laws of light and shade, though the preliminary investigations of Piero della Francesca deserve to be recorded.

He observed with strict accuracy the subtleties of chiaroscuro—light and shade apart from colour; but, as one critic has pointed out, his gift of chiaroscuro cost the colour-life of many a noble picture. Leonardo was "a tonist, not a colourist," before whom the whole book of nature lay open.

It was not instability of character but versatility of mind which caused him to undertake many things that having commenced he afterwards abandoned, and the probability is that as soon as he saw exactly how he could solve any difficulty which presented itself, he put on one side the merely perfunctory execution of such a task.

In the Forster collection in the Victoria and Albert museum three of Leonardo's note-books with sketches are preserved, and it is stated that it was his practice to carry about with him, attached to his girdle, a little book for making sketches. They prove that he was left-handed and wrote from right to left.

HIS MIND

We can readily believe the statements of Benvenuto Cellini, the sixteenth-century Goldsmith, that Francis I. "did not believe that any other man had come into the world who had attained so great a knowledge as Leonardo, and that not only as sculptor, painter, and architect, for beyond that he was a profound philosopher." It was Cellini also who contended that "Leonardo da Vinci, Michelangelo, and Raphael are the Book of the World."

Leonardo anticipated many eminent scientists and inventors in the methods of investigation which they adopted to solve the many problems with which their names are coupled. Among these may be cited Copernicus' theory of the earth's movement, Lamarck's classification of vertebrate and invertebrate animals, the laws of friction, the laws of combustion and respiration, the elevation of the continents, the laws of gravitation, the undulatory theory of light and heat, steam as a motive power in navigation, flying machines, the invention of the camera obscura, magnetic attraction, the use of the stone saw, the system of canalisation, breech loading cannon, the construction of fortifications, the circulation of the blood, the swimming belt, the wheelbarrow, the composition of explosives, the invention of paddle wheels, the smoke stack, the mincing machine! It is, therefore, easy to see why he called "Mechanics the Paradise of the Sciences."

Leonardo was a SUPERMAN.

HIS MAXIMS

The eye is the window of the soul.

Tears come from the heart and not from the brain.

The natural desire of good men is knowledge.

A beautiful body perishes, but a work of art dies not.

Every difficulty can be overcome by effort.

Time abides long enough for those who make use of it.

Miserable men, how often do you enslave yourselves   to gain money!

HIS SPELL

The influence of Leonardo was strongly felt in Milan, where he spent so many of the best years of his life and founded a School of painting. He was a close observer of the gradation and reflex of light, and was capable of giving to his discoveries a practical and aesthetic form. His strong personal character and the fascination of his genius enthralled his followers, who were satisfied to repeat his types, to perpetuate the "grey-hound eye," and to make use of his little devices. Among this group of painters may be mentioned Boltraffio, who perhaps painted the

"Presumed Portrait of Lucrezia Crivelli" (VII.), which is officially attributed in the Louvre to the great master himself.

HIS
DESCENDANTS

Signor Uzielli has shown that one Tommaso da Vinci, a descendant of Domenico (one of Leonardo's brothers), was a few years ago a peasant at Bottinacio near Montespertoli, and had then in his possession the family papers, which now form part of the archives of the Accademia dei Lincei at Rome. It was proved also that Tommaso had given his eldest son "the glorious name of Leonardo."

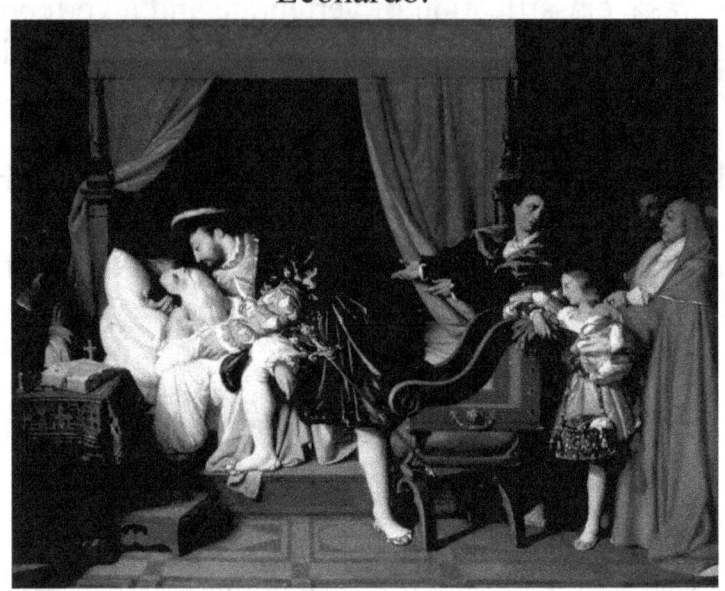

Death Of Leonardo Da Vinci--Jean Auguste Dominique Ingres--1818

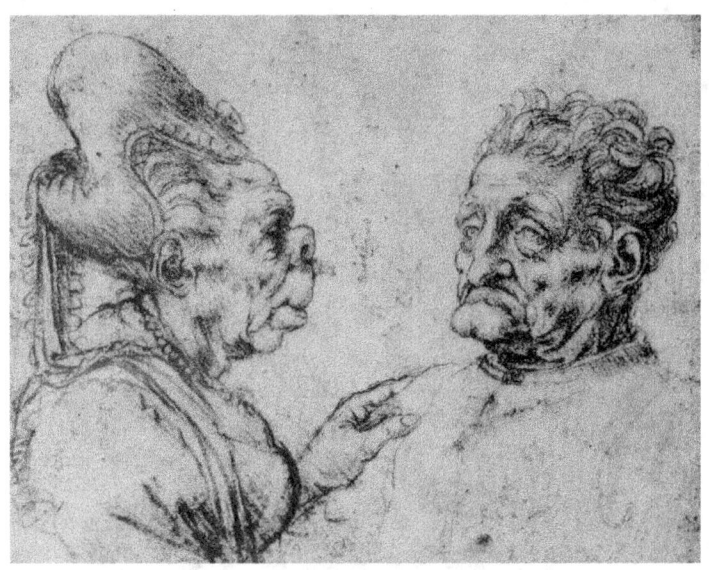

Caricature

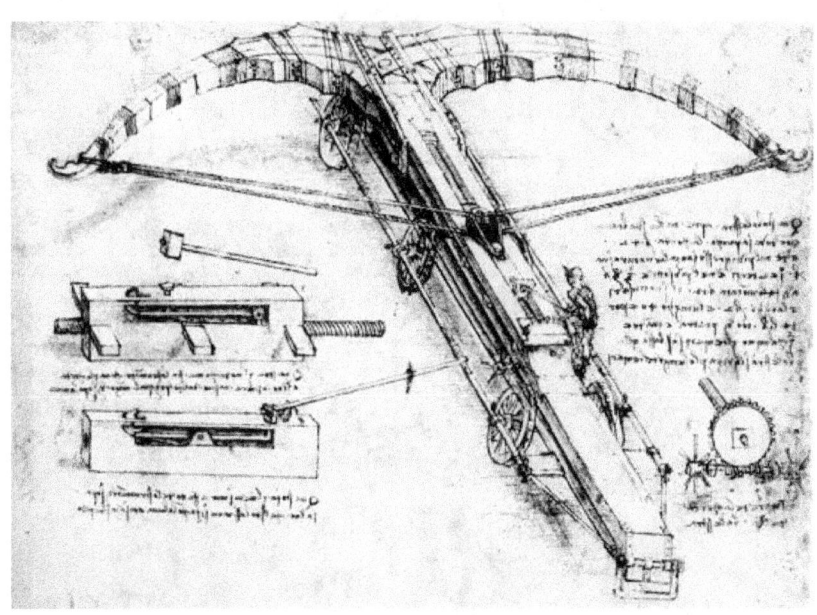

Design For A Giant Crossbow--1482

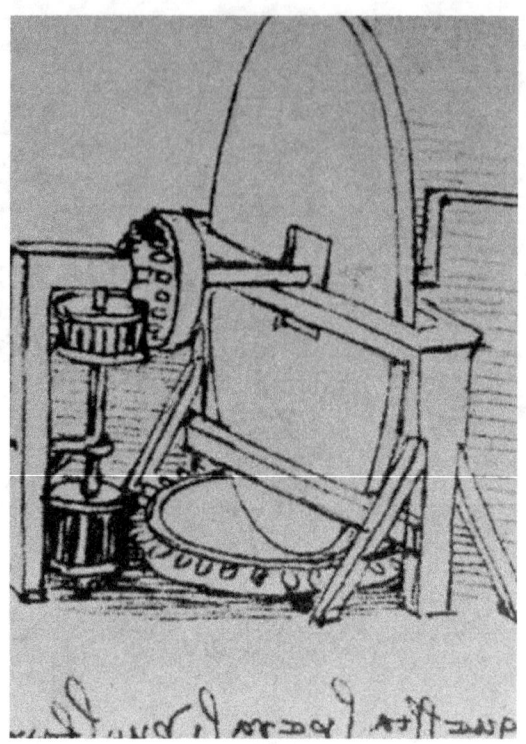

Design For A Machine For Grinding Convex Lenses--1500

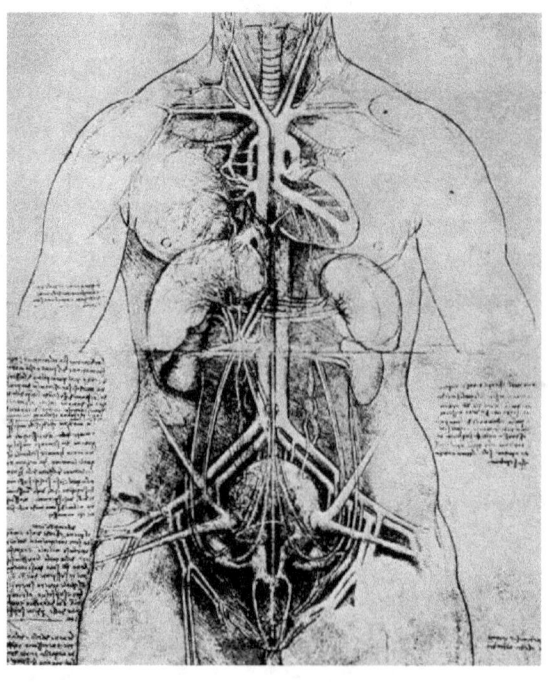

Drawing Of A Woman's Torso

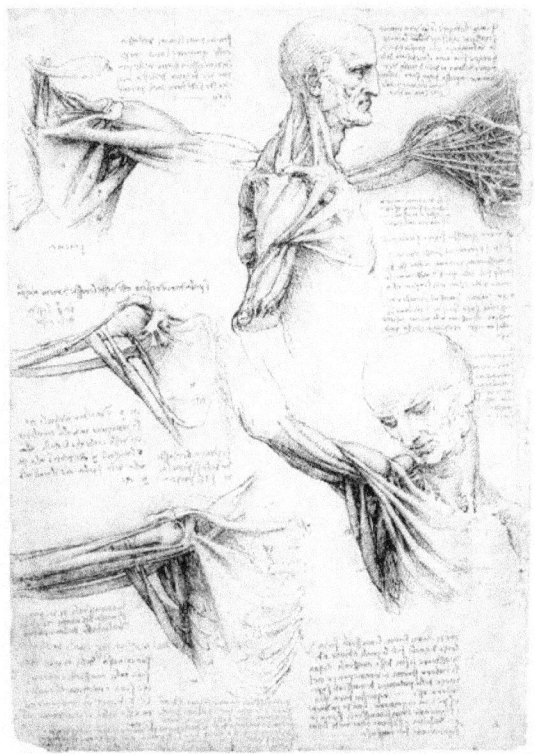

Anatomical Studies Of The Shoulder--1510

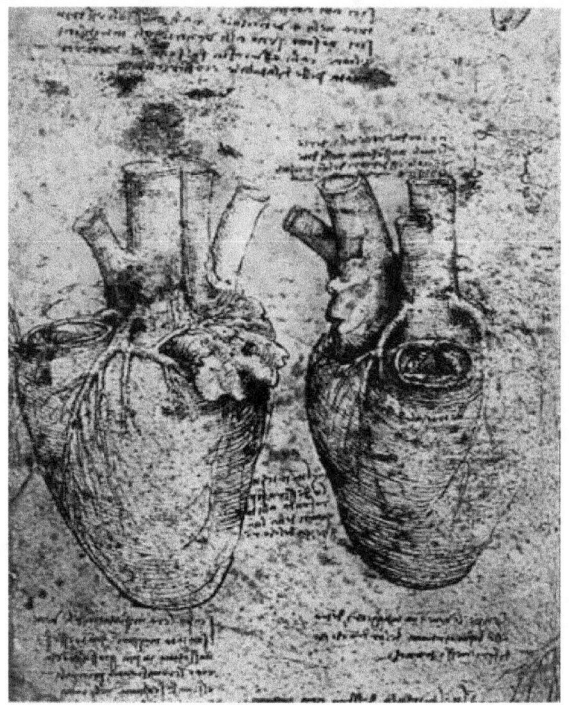

Heart and its Blood Vessels